Wee God Moments of Meditation

Moving Mountains Through Crumbs of Faith

Journal

CAROL TURNBOUGH

Published by So It Is Written, LLC
Detroit, MI
SoItIsWritten.net

Wee God Moments of Meditation: Moving Mountains through Crumbs of Faith Journal
Copyright © 2023 by Carol Turnbough

Edited by: So It Is Written – www.SoItIsWritten.net

Formatting by: Ya Ya Ya Creative – www.YaYaYaCreative.com

ISBN: 979-8-9861260-8-1

PRINTED AND BOUND IN THE UNITED STATES OF AMERICA

This *Journal*
Belongs To:

_____

In difficult, challenging moments, praise Him!
In happy, joyful moments, praise Him!
In all moments of moments, praise Him!
Praise Him!
Praise Him!

Let everything that has breath and every breath of life praise the LORD! Praise The LORD! (Psalm 150:6).

Meditation Moments:

_____

_____

_____

_____

_____

_____

_____

_____

_____

_____

_____

_____

_____

_____

_____

_____

_____

_____

_____

_____

_____

_____

_____

_____

_____

_____

_____

_____

_____

_____

Live each day as if it's your last. Be appreciative of
what the Lord has done. Let each hour allow
you to bring a smile to someone's lips and heart.

Remember J.O.Y.

Jesus, Others, and You!

Meditation Moments:

_____

_____

_____

_____

_____

_____

_____

_____

_____

_____

_____

_____

_____

_____

_____

_____

_____

_____

As time graciously unfolds, keep in mind the grace of Jesus. His grace never changes. It remains the same forever. May grace burst from your lips, with peace flooding your heart and soul.

Meditation Moments:

Don't withdraw your kindness to protect yourself from being taken for granted. Instead, go overboard showing His kindness, and it will return to you with a mighty windfall.

Meditation Moments:

Take a few moments to express gratitude for the many things you have that you didn't pray for.

Don't let this day go by
without giving Him great praise!

Meditation Moments:

_____

_____

_____

_____

_____

_____

_____

_____

_____

_____

_____

_____

_____

_____

Keep His Word hidden in your heart while He orders your steps to brighten the path. He constantly blesses us with His tender mercy.

Living out biblical principles is mandated, and we must read, study and meditate on the Word.

Meditation Moments:

_____

_____

_____

_____

_____

_____

_____

_____

_____

_____

_____

_____

_____

_____

When you know who you are, you can keep your focus on
God's purpose, plan and prize for your life.

*Stay faithful to your
appointment with a passion.*

*Meditation
Moments:* _____

_____

_____

_____

_____

_____

_____

_____

_____

_____

_____

_____

_____

_____

_____

_____

Don't get distracted by the natural things
of life and neglect the spiritual things of
life that are yours for the asking.

Meditation Moments:

_____

_____

_____

_____

_____

_____

_____

_____

_____

_____

_____

_____

_____

_____

_____

_____

_____

_____

Decide to be a vessel through which God works.

If you are broken and shattered into a million hideous pieces, it doesn't matter.

Jesus said, "Come as you are."

Come to me, all you who are weary and burdened, and I will give you rest. (Matthew 11:28)

Meditation Moments:

_____

_____

_____

_____

_____

_____

_____

_____

_____

_____

_____

_____

_____

_____

_____

_____

Circumstances may knock you down.

The good news is you don't have to stay down.

The Lord always has a way for
you to get up and return with favor.

Meditation Moments:

_____

_____

_____

_____

_____

_____

_____

_____

_____

_____

_____

_____

_____

_____

_____

_____

_____

_____

_____

_____

_____

_____

_____

_____

_____

_____

_____

_____

_____

_____

_____

_____

_____

_____

_____

_____

Waiting, with patience added to the mix, helps you to see bona fide, genuine integrity and character.

Meditation Moments: _____

_____

_____

_____

_____

_____

_____

_____

_____

_____

_____

_____

_____

_____

_____

_____

_____

_____

_____

_____

_____

May the love of Jesus keep you looking beyond the past.

Although things may seem sorrowful and discouraging, keep walking in faith's path.

The glow of Christ will lead you through the valley.

Meditation Moments:

_____

_____

_____

_____

_____

_____

_____

_____

_____

_____

_____

_____

_____

_____

_____

_____

Oh, how wonderful it is when the Holy One lives inside of you! Be thankful that He has chosen you to bring His glory to the world. He is doing a great work and supplying all our needs according to His riches in glory, and He needs you to tell it.

Meditation Moments:

_____

_____

_____

_____

_____

_____

_____

_____

_____

_____

_____

_____

_____

_____

_____

_____

_____

_____

The Lord has forgiven us.

We have no reason to hold
onto anything we have done.

*The One whose words are the most important
deemed you righteous, clean and holy.*

Meditation Moments:

_____

_____

_____

_____

_____

_____

_____

_____

_____

_____

_____

_____

_____

_____

_____

_____

Cry out to God with a whisper
to keep working on you.

> *When it's time to go forward, look up and*
> *keep your mouth and lips in His hands.*

God has all you want and need.

Meditation Moments:

_____

_____

_____

_____

_____

_____

_____

_____

_____

_____

_____

_____

_____

_____

_____

_____

_____

_____

God's goodness endures forever.

There is nothing like being an energized believer.

You never stop running or
jumping for the great Jehovah.

But, if you get down, cry to Him,
for He understands the language of tears.

Even Jesus wept.

Meditation Moments:

_____

_____

_____

_____

_____

_____

_____

_____

_____

_____

_____

_____

Take these shoes off … being critical, overly religious, irritated, disobedient, and seeing yourself as less than how God sees you. Instead, slip on the running slippers of right godly living. They are much more comfortable.

Meditation Moments: _____

_____

_____

_____

_____

_____

_____

_____

_____

_____

_____

_____

_____

_____

_____

_____

_____

_____

In the middle of being strong, you may fall.

Acknowledge your failure as you pray.
Look at what led to the failure. Learn from it. Use that
failure to prevent it from reoccurring in the future.

Then, pray some more.

Meditation
Moments: _____

_____

_____

_____

_____

_____

_____

_____

_____

_____

_____

_____

_____

_____

Ask the Holy Spirit what lies and secret sins you are believing about yourself.

Believe the report of the Lord.

His report proclaims that you are free and have victory.

Who can understand his errors? Cleanse thou me from secret faults. Keep your servant from deliberate sins. Don't let them control me. Then I will be free of guilt and innocent of great sin. (Psalm 19:12-13)

Meditation Moments:

_____

_____

_____

_____

_____

_____

_____

_____

_____

_____

_____

_____

_____

_____

_____

_____

_____

_____

_____

_____

_____

_____

_____

_____

_____

_____

_____

_____

Glory to the Lord! We are abundantly blessed to have what God wants us to have. We are also blessed not to have what God has not allowed. May our desires stay tuned in to God's holy writ.

Meditation Moments:

The love of God isn't based on what we say or do,
but on the fact that He is love!

That's the pure essence of who
and what God *is* and *does.*

Even when we deem His correction as tough love.

Meditation
Moments: _____

_____

_____

_____

_____

_____

_____

_____

_____

_____

_____

_____

_____

_____

_____

_____

_____

_____

_____

_____

_____

_____

_____

_____

_____

_____

_____

_____

_____

_____

_____

_____

_____

_____

Don't get trapped in a weary period of your life,
longing to find something to do.

Instead, keep seeking answers for spiritual insight
and take advantage of this quiet time.

God is always present in still moments.

He is stretching your faith; therefore,
stand still and see the salvation of the Lord.

Meditation
Moments:

_____

_____

_____

_____

_____

_____

_____

_____

_____

_____

_____

_____

_____

_____

_____

_____

_____

_____

_____

_____

_____

_____

_____

_____

_____

_____

_____

_____

_____

_____

_____

If you think about things that only remind you of the good old days, life can make you feel stagnant.

Don't just live to get by.

According to Philippians 4:8, Make up your mind, and renew your attitude with *things that are true, honest, just, pure, lovely, and of a good report.*

───────※◇═◇═◇═◇◇═───────

Meditation Moments: _____

_____

_____

_____

_____

_____

_____

_____

_____

_____

_____

_____

_____

_____

_____

_____

_____

_____

_____

_____

_____

_____

_____

_____

_____

_____

_____

_____

_____

_____

_____

_____

How we treat the Word of God is how we treat God.

God and the Word (Jesus) are one and the same.

Meditation Moments:

_____

_____

_____

_____

_____

_____

_____

_____

_____

_____

_____

_____

_____

_____

_____

_____

Psalm 90:12,14 tells us that when we learn to number our days early with Jehovah-Rohi, we are able to apply our hearts unto wisdom, rejoice and be glad all our days.

Meditation Moments:

_____

_____

_____

_____

_____

_____

_____

_____

_____

_____

_____

_____

_____

_____

_____

Jesus is our Lord and Savior.

He guides us with His mighty power.

Without Him, we are nothing.

But, with Him, we can be the champions He has called us
to be with confidence and honesty.

Meditation Moments:

_____

_____

_____

_____

_____

_____

_____

_____

_____

_____

_____

_____

_____

_____

We are in a battle with the One who thinks he holds the world in his hands. Ephesians 6:12 tells us that our battle is ... *not against flesh and blood, but against principalities, against powers, against the rulers of the darkness of this world, against spiritual wickedness in high places.*

As believers, we must let the
Word of God fight our battles.

Meditation Moments:

_____

_____

_____

_____

_____

_____

_____

_____

_____

_____

_____

_____

_____

_____

_____

Pray. Sow. Get yourself ready for the overflow.

*God can do anything, you know—far more
than you could ever imagine or guess or request
in your wildest dreams.* (Ephesians 3:20)

*Meditation
Moments:* _____

_____

_____

_____

_____

_____

_____

_____

_____

_____

_____

_____

_____

_____

_____

_____

_____

_____

Allow God's Spirit to lead, guide, and direct your way.

We can't so easily become stressed, confused, or anxious when we feel ourselves on a downward slope.

There is always hope in He Who has complete control.

***

Meditation Moments:

_____

_____

_____

_____

_____

_____

_____

_____

_____

_____

_____

_____

_____

_____

_____

_____

_____

Humble yourself in knowing that the King is on the throne of your heart. You are so pleasing to Him, and your living is not in vain. Don't let flesh and blood dethrone the King in you.

Meditation Moments:

Leap over walls of bitterness.

Embrace your victory!

Be enlightened, enriched,
equipped and encouraged.

Meditation Moments:

_____

_____

_____

_____

_____

_____

_____

_____

_____

_____

_____

_____

_____

_____

_____

_____

_____

Reach out and touch someone with the strength He has given you so they can have someone to lean on.

The Lord is your strength and power: He makes your way perfect. (2 Samuel 22:33)

Meditation Moments:

_____

_____

_____

_____

_____

_____

_____

_____

_____

_____

_____

_____

_____

_____

_____

_____

You have been at this stop many times before.

Each time, you recognize surrendering is long overdue.

Come with your heart and hands up.

You are complete in Him.

You desperately need to spend more
time with Jesus to pass the test.

Meditation
Moments: _____

_____

_____

_____

_____

_____

_____

_____

_____

_____

_____

_____

_____

_____

Time out for being a hearer only of the Word.
We must be doers.

If you don't live it, it's not beneficial for
yourself, others, or Christ.

It's like walking in absolute darkness every day,
never knowing if or when you will fall.

But, through the Word of God,
you can rise stronger.

Meditation
Moments:

Why keep trying to convince God to do something
for you when He's already given the victory to you?

Lift up your hands and
take hold of the promises.

They are still right there with you,
just waiting for you to enjoy.

Meditation
Moments: _____
_____

_____

_____

_____

_____

_____

_____

_____

_____

_____

_____

_____

_____

_____

We belong to Jesus, who paid the price with His life.

The only way we can repay God for what
His beloved Son has done is to give complete
control of everything back to Him.

*Meditation
Moments:*

Why become more satisfied with crutches than Christ?

You have the ability to move without knowing all the answers. Faith is moving without knowing which way to go.

> *Greater is He that is in you*
> *than He that is in the world.*
> (1 John 4:4)

Meditation Moments:

_____

_____

_____

_____

_____

_____

_____

_____

_____

_____

_____

_____

_____

One key to great success is your authenticity for the Lord.

Never forget how wonderful and awesome He is and will always be.

Don't worry about being deep. Just be real!

Meditation Moments:

_____

_____

_____

_____

_____

_____

_____

_____

_____

_____

_____

_____

_____

_____

_____

_____

_____

_____

_____

_____

_____

_____

_____

_____

_____

_____

_____

_____

_____

_____

_____

_____

_____

_____

Forget about the past and concentrate on the future. Forgive yourself. We all make mistakes, errors, and blunders. We all fall short of the glory of our Heavenly Father. It's impossible to become an excellent driver by looking out the back window as you drive. You got me?

Meditation Moments:

_____

_____

_____

_____

_____

_____

_____

_____

_____

_____

_____

_____

_____

_____

As we travel through this barren land,
which is not our home,
never forget that you are either
going through or coming out.

Remember His Word.

Pray the Word.

Say the Word.

You will taste and see that the Lord is good.

Meditation Moments:

_____

_____

_____

_____

_____

_____

_____

_____

_____

Release through prayer, His strength.

Release through thanksgiving, His power.

Release through praise, His anointing.

Be willing to obey and do whatever it takes to let go.

God is the order of your life.

Meditation Moments:

We are not perfect, but we are being perfected.

We must trust Him to deliver us to those things that are best and deliver us from those things that are not.

Give us this day our daily bread, Lord!

Meditation Moments:

Love is contagious when it is our number one priority.

People see our joy and the goodness of
Shekinah Glory, which is how love illuminates.

Meditation
Moments:

Sit at the well with Jesus. His living water will bubble over in your soul. He will keep revealing "your stuff" so you can keep fighting with His authority and power. Remember, you are in a win-win situation.

Meditation Moments:

When good happens, and
it comes to fruition, it's God.

Don't take credit for anything
good that happens to you.

God will keep working on your behalf
as you trust Him with all your heart,
leaning not on your own understanding.

Meditation
Moments:

_____

_____

_____

_____

_____

_____

_____

_____

_____

_____

_____

The Almighty One is on your side.

No matter what this day may bring, have great joy.

It's great peace to know you are in His loving care.

There is nothing He doesn't know about before it happens.

You are safe in the Redeemer's arms.

Meditation Moments:

_____

_____

_____

_____

_____

_____

_____

_____

_____

_____

_____

_____

Still searching for how to overcome physically,
emotionally, mentally and spiritually?

Stay renewed in your mind through the spirit.

Your faith and belief will hold up,
placing you on a firm foundation when
it feels like you are falling apart and sinking.

Meditation Moments: _____

_____

_____

_____

_____

_____

_____

_____

_____

_____

_____

_____

_____

As seasons change, things must change.

Life forces change,
whether you like it or not.

Recognize that changes rapidly come
for your growth and for your good.

Meditation Moments:

_____

_____

_____

_____

_____

_____

_____

_____

_____

_____

_____

_____

_____

_____

_____

_____

The Holy Spirit has filled us with His zeal and energy.
We don't have to bow under the weight of the world.

"Thou shall not have other gods outside of me."
(Exodus 20:3)

Meditation
Moments:

_____

_____

_____

_____

_____

_____

_____

_____

_____

_____

_____

_____

_____

_____

Thank the Lord *for your cup, which keeps running over with goodness, mercy and grace.*

Thank Him *for anointing your head with oil, authority, power and wisdom.*

Thank Him *for always being present and providing you riches for the body and spirit.*

Meditation Moments: _____

_____

_____

_____

_____

_____

_____

_____

_____

_____

_____

_____

_____

_____

_____

The enemy seeks to gain a foothold in our lives.

His aim is to get the believer off focus from
worshipping the true and living God.

*Therefore, declare daily he will not
steal your joy, peace or love.*

*We stand on the promises of the
living God, which are forever.*

*Meditation
Moments:*

God, you are awesome and anointed.

You are the Bread of Life, compassionate deliverer, eternal, faithful, good, great, holy, impartial, just, kind, loving, merciful, near, omnipresent, powerful, righteous, sovereign, trustworthy, unchanging, victorious, worthy and excellent.

Yahweh, you are so much more.

Meditation Moments:

_____

_____

_____

_____

_____

_____

_____

_____

_____

_____

_____

_____

_____

_____

_____

_____

Do you know what God thinks about you?

Loves about you?

Take the time to list them.

Meditation Moments:

_____

_____

_____

_____

_____

_____

_____

_____

_____

_____

_____

_____

_____

_____

_____

_____

_____

_____

You may experience warfare of the mind, attacks in the spirit and flesh, as the cares of this world make you think you are alone. But the Lord's love is carrying you under His wings. Nothing and no one can separate you from His love. Absolutely nothing can get between us and God's love because of how Jesus, our Master, has embraced us.

(Romans 8:39)

Meditation Moments:

Before we speak, it's done.

God honors the spoken word.

So, we must open our mouths wide,
with lifted hands and hearts,
speaking His Word that has been
delegated by the authority of Jesus Christ.

Meditation
Moments:

Be all in with the Holy Spirit.

His will becomes the standard.

...The spirit of the Lord will lift up a standard against him and put him to flight. (Isaiah 59:19)

Meditation Moments:

_____

_____

_____

_____

_____

_____

_____

_____

_____

_____

_____

_____

_____

_____

_____

_____

You were designed with an unstoppable spirit to be bold, confident and authentic.

Even when God's purpose isn't always clear to you, know that the Lord will fulfill His purpose for your life.

He's got a God plan for good things.

Meditation Moments:

_____

_____

_____

_____

_____

_____

_____

_____

_____

_____

_____

_____

_____

_____

_____

_____

Slow down, pause, and
take time to do a self-examination.

If you are slipping back to that
place of, "Never again!" stop!

You will hear the Lord calling you
back to Him softly and tenderly.

He helps you stay in a
blissful and holy space

Meditation Moments:

_____

_____

_____

_____

_____

_____

_____

_____

_____

Don't use your words to tear down, offend or bring shame to the kingdom of God. Instead, speech should be used to uplift and encourage others. Our faithful Master gave us the gift of speech to uplift, honor, adore and bless Him.

Meditation Moments:

_____

_____

_____

_____

_____

_____

_____

_____

_____

_____

_____

_____

_____

We all have seasons of weeping, which does not always mean tears are involved.

But, when the enemy comes to kill, steal and destroy, the weeping or feeling sorry for yourself, of loving the cares and concerns of this world more than the things of the spirit, of holding on and not giving, keeps us in a weeping position longer than we need to be.

Meditation Moments:

_____

_____

_____

_____

_____

_____

_____

_____

_____

_____

_____

Open your arms wide to receive blessings.

Then, shower them on someone else,
giving God glory, honor, and praise.

More of Him; less of you.

Get the wisdom to understand that
it's not about what you want,
but what the Father wants for your good.

Meditation Moments:

_____

_____

_____

_____

_____

_____

_____

_____

_____

_____

_____

Be guilty of being a cheerful giver as you are blessed to bless others. Declare what goes out will return 100-fold!

Remember this: Whoever sows sparingly will also reap sparingly, and whoever sows generously will also reap generously. (2 Corinthians 9:6)

Meditation Moments: _____

_____

_____

_____

_____

_____

_____

_____

_____

_____

_____

_____

_____

_____

_____

_____

Christ Jesus is our Lord, the One from Whom we seek guidance for our life's journey. Without Him, we are nothing. With Him, we can be the individuals He has chosen us to be. Having His desires and passions, according to 1 Peter 2:9, drive us to be ...*a peculiar people; that should shew forth the praises of Him who hath called us out of darkness into His marvelous light.*

Meditation Moments:

You may have heard the saying, "It is what it is."

So, to us who have our hope in the name of the Lord, "It is what it is in Christ."

You must stand on Christ, the Solid Rock.

All other ground is sinking sand.

Meditation Moments:

Let the redeemed of the Lord give it up
to the author and finisher of their faith!

Offer up the sacrifices of praise.

With such sacrifices, El-Roi is pleased!

He hath shewed thee, O man, what is good; and what doth
the Lord require of thee, but to do justly, and to love mercy,
and to walk humbly with thy God? (Micah 6:8)

Meditation Moments:

_____

_____

_____

_____

_____

_____

_____

_____

_____

_____

_____

_____

If you notice the struggles in your soul are making
headlines, fellowship more with God.

When you see answered prayers coming forth,
ask for a wider lens for a better view.

Then, go back to claim what was missed.

Every promise in the Bible is yours.

Meditation Moments:

The shadows in the valley tend to make us lean on our own understanding, looking for a quick getaway.

The Holy One tells us to
put on the full armor.

Only then can we escape with great victory.

Meditation Moments:

_____

_____

_____

_____

_____

_____

_____

_____

_____

_____

_____

_____

_____

_____

If we stay in the posture of disobedience,
we will never know how disconnected and
out of fellowship we are from the Father.

According to Isaiah 1:19, if we will only obey
and let Him help us, we will reap the
blessed benefits.

Meditation Moments:

_____

_____

_____

_____

_____

_____

_____

_____

_____

_____

_____

_____

_____

Be in everything to win.

We have been placed in certain lanes to
totally depend on Jehovah Jireh,
the winner of everything,
whose worth is priceless.

Meditation
Moments: _____

_____

_____

_____

_____

_____

_____

_____

_____

_____

_____

_____

_____

_____

_____

_____

Stay in the realm of the Master.

God is still working on you.

You are to do His will, not your own agenda.

Meditation Moments:

_____

_____

Steady your focus on your assignment.

You are duty-bound to help someone grow and press onward.

Kind and sweet words on your lips will
heal wounds and cover a multitude of sins.

Meditation
Moments:

Feeling lonely and wondering what's your next move? That's not a bad thing. In fact, it's a blessed thing to be alone when it lands you at the top with the Holy Spirit, with just you and God.

Meditation Moments:

_____

_____

_____

_____

_____

_____

_____

_____

_____

_____

_____

_____

_____

_____

_____

_____

_____

_____

_____

_____

Keep your mind stayed on Jesus,
even after hearing things that try to
bring heaviness and burdens to your soul.

Hold on to your desires;
they will bring you feelings of
joy in times of, "Why me?"

Meditation Moments:

_____

_____

_____

_____

_____

_____

_____

_____

_____

_____

_____

_____

Jesus loves us with an everlasting love.

He only wants obedience to whatever brings
you closer to Him because it pleases God.

He separated you from your mother's womb
and called you by His grace.

That is love!

Meditation Moments:

_____

_____

_____

_____

_____

_____

_____

_____

_____

_____

_____

_____

_____

_____

Draw closer and closer to God through Christ Jesus.

He will reveal in and through you
even more of His treasures.

Where your treasure is, there your heart will be also.
(Matthew 6:21)

Meditation Moments:

_____

_____

_____

_____

_____

_____

_____

_____

_____

_____

_____

_____

_____

_____

_____

_____

_____

We are beautifully made inside and out.

We are God's workmanship.

Stand still, examine yourself from
top to bottom, and see you are amazing.

He only creates the top of the line.

Meditation
Moments:

_____

_____

_____

_____

_____

_____

_____

_____

_____

_____

_____

_____

_____

_____

Praise the Lord for entering your life. He gave you the eyes to see and ears to hear. He gave you a voice to spread His gospel and comfort others. He even gave you strength to sing His praise in your heart and out loud in cheerful and rough times.

Meditation Moments:

Oppositions will become opportunities.

Thank the Lord when you fall
into diverse temptations.

*God has brought you through
situations in the past, and
He will bring you through again.*

Meditation
Moments:

_____

_____

_____

_____

_____

_____

_____

_____

_____

_____

_____

_____

_____

_____

_____

_____

_____

_____

_____

_____

_____

_____

_____

_____

_____

_____

_____

_____

_____

_____

_____

_____

Look with purpose.

Stop looking at the little foxes
that are trying to claim your attention,
courage, and vitality.

Let the Trinity re-group you.

───────◆──◇──◆───────

Meditation Moments:

_____

_____

_____

_____

_____

_____

_____

_____

_____

_____

_____

_____

_____

_____

_____

Once lost, but now walking in the light.

Once a sinner, but now saved with a transformed heart and soul.

You can't help but rejoice with unspeakable joy.

Meditation Moments:

The worst things turn out to be the things that will propel you to your destiny and build you into the person you were created for.

Meditation Moments:

It's not meant for us to get stuck in a hard, hopeless place. Give El Shaddai all the what-nots and what-fors. I guarantee you He will reshape what has been shattered and taken away.

Meditation Moments:

When looking with your eyes at the things of God,
you never see the full view.

What will happen, how, and when are best kept
with the Owner Who made your soul.

If you knew the answers,
you might try to replace God.

Meditation
Moments: _____

_____

_____

_____

_____

_____

_____

_____

_____

_____

_____

_____

_____

_____

No matter what it takes, the Lord can do it for you.

Be willing and obedient to receive a windfall of increased spiritual and material blessings.

Prepare to be used for His service.

Meditation Moments:

Shout out to you!

Be happy!

Be joyful!

Be your unique special self.

No one can replace you.

If you could be replaced, there would be no you.

I will praise thee: for I am fearfully and wonderfully made: marvelous are thy works; and that my soul knoweth right well. (Psalm 139:14)

Meditation Moments:

_____

_____

_____

_____

_____

_____

_____

_____

_____

_____

_____

Lord, You have given us the
assurance that if we speak
to any mountain in faith,
it shall be moved in Your timing,
Your way, and for Your glory.

When we send Your Word,
it will accomplish that
which it was sent to do.

Meditation Moments:

_____

_____

_____

_____

_____

_____

_____

_____

_____

_____

_____

_____

_____

_____

_____

No weapon will prosper against us because You have given
Your angels charge over us to keep us.

Therefore, we humbly petition You to
give us the wisdom to plead the
blood of Jesus over our houses,
to keep the diseases out,
but give us peace,
healing and protection.

Meditation
Moments:

_____

_____

_____

_____

_____

_____

_____

_____

_____

_____

_____

_____

_____

_____

_____

_____

_____

_____

_____

_____

_____

God is all in all! He is an awesome, mighty God. Yet, He calls us His! Thank Him for His everlasting grace, love and mercy, which is new every day! Thank Him for putting His love in us so we can share with others as we proclaim His goodness through the written Word, through our voices, and through our righteous living!

Meditation Moments:

_____

_____

_____

_____

_____

_____

_____

_____

_____

_____

About the Author

While many people "make a joyful noise unto the Lord" figuratively, she is the walking epitome of that verse. Affectionately known as "Song of Joy," Carol Turnbough has ministered through music and writing for more than fifty years. Touching the hearts of children and youth of all ages, and even those young at heart, her passion for praise is contagious to all she may encounter—in and outside the four walls of the traditional church. Empowered by God's love, grace, and mercy, Carol has been abundantly blessed with many spiritual gifts, including the gift of teaching, helps, songs and administration, to name a few.

Recognized most over the years for her dedication and commitment to the children and other ministries at Messiah Baptist Church in Detroit, Carol first used writing as a method to easily remember Scriptures and teach them to children. When she became a teacher in the public-school system, it only made sense for her to use that same skillset to motivate students by song, journaling and children's stories. Endowed with a persuasive, encouraging spirit,

Carol is on a mission to spread one simple message: God is all you need, but you must trust and believe in Him.

Adamant about making her boast in the Lord, Carol also holds a Bachelor of Arts from Marygrove College, as well as a Master of Arts from University of Detroit Mercy. In addition to her ministerial and educational accolades, Carol boasts proudly of her marriage of more than forty-two years to the love of her life, Javan Turnbough, which yielded three children and five grandchildren to date.

For more information or booking, email
cturn1950@aol.com or call 313.815.6805.